**CCSS** Genre Realistic Ficti...

 Y0-DAB-077

 Essential Question
What kinds of challenges transform people?

Bear Country

by Susan Paris
illustrated by Aleksandar Sotirovski

Chapter 1 Baggage

Frankie sat on the sofa reading a book. She was trying to **concentrate**, but it was hard to keep her mind on the story. Her younger brother, Lee, was hitting the sofa with his tennis racket. Thwack! Thwack! Thwack!

Frankie ignored her brother. If she kept reading quietly, he might give up and go away.

"You don't *have* to come hiking with us," Lee whispered angrily. "Why don't you spend the day with your friend Audrey?"

It was a good idea. Frankie didn't even want to go on the hiking trip. A few months ago, Dad had suggested taking Lee and his friends hiking in Rocky Mountain National Park. It was supposed to be a boys-only trip, and Frankie's mom was going to take her to the aquarium. But Mom had to go on a business trip, and this left Frankie without plans. Now Frankie felt like unwanted baggage.

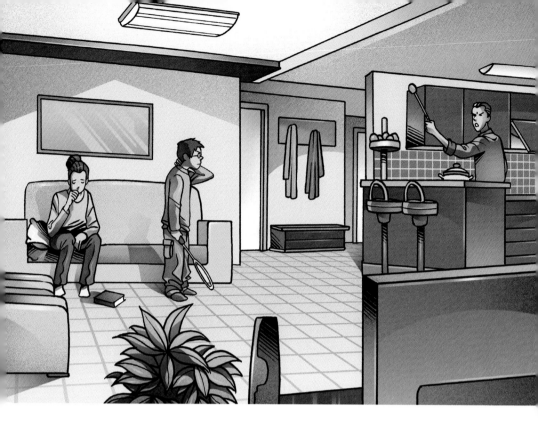

"I'll get the phone so you can call Audrey," Lee said. Frankie wished he would leave her alone and stop being so **persistent**.

"Lee!" Dad called from the kitchen. "We've discussed this. Frankie's coming on the hiking trip, and that's final."

Now Frankie was mad, too. The truth was that she'd much rather *read* about hiking in Rocky Mountain National Park than actually *go* hiking. She didn't want to spend the day with her brother and his annoying friends, and most of all she didn't want to meet any bears.

The next morning, when Lee's friends Damien and Adam arrived, Frankie was standing by the car. They didn't seem surprised to see her. Lee had probably sent them texts complaining about her.

"You all need to check your own supplies," Dad said. "Make sure that you have water, food, extra clothes, and a raincoat." Frankie and the boys did what Dad asked and checked their gear.

Frankie watched as Dad checked his own supplies. He had everything they might need: compass, survival blanket, first-aid kit, extra water, matches, and more.

Finally, they were ready to go. Lee and his friends climbed into the back seat and immediately started listening to music and telling jokes. "I bet they wouldn't notice if Dad were driving them to the moon," Frankie thought. She was the only one who looked out the window at the trees, mountains, and other **scenery**. Dad was happy that she seemed interested in the trip.

"Look at that!" he said, pointing at the view. "No malls or traffic jams—just us and the great outdoors."

STOP AND CHECK

Why does Frankie have to go on the hike?

Dad wanted to make sure they got into the real outdoors on their hiking trip. He had chosen one of the least popular hiking trails, which began at the end of an **isolated** road. Dad was happy that there were only a few people around.

"We'll have the place to ourselves," he said, and he dropped his gear on the ground.

Frankie felt a little uneasy, but all she said to her dad was, "Do you have a map?"

"Of course," Dad said. "Let's take a look. I'll show you where we're going." Frankie felt a little more relaxed once she and her dad had studied the map.

It was raining a little when they started hiking. The trail stretched before them and disappeared into the forest like a path in a fairy tale.

The boys wanted to run ahead, but Dad insisted that they must all stay together. "Safety in numbers," he said.

"Safety from what?" Frankie asked nervously.

"Bears," Adam said. "They're all over these woods."

Frankie *knew* she should have refused to go on this trip and gone to Audrey's house instead.

"They're just black bears," Damien said. "They'll leave you alone if you're careful."

"True," Dad said. "Never approach a bear, and make lots of noise when you're hiking so you don't surprise one. If you do see one, tell me right away."

"That's right, Frankie," Lee said. "Make sure you tell Dad right before you start running from the big, bad bear's claws and teeth." Lee growled like a bear, and he pretended to swipe at Frankie with his outstretched arms.

Frankie jumped with fear, and Lee and the other boys laughed at her.

"That's enough, Lee," Dad said sternly. "Frankie, you lead the way."

"Do I have to?" Frankie asked. "I don't want to be in the front."

"Okay," Dad said. "I'll lead the way, but let's get going."

They walked steadily uphill and the day brightened around them. They saw nothing but trees, a hawk, and the bright blue sky. Once in a while, they saw some **magnificent** mountains between the trees, but Frankie couldn't enjoy the impressive view. She was trying to keep up with the others and not trip over any rocks. So far, she was doing okay. And most importantly, they hadn't seen any bears.

When they reached a clearing, Dad announced that it was lunchtime. They had climbed surprisingly high. Frankie gazed at the **vastness** of the landscape, which stretched as far as she could see. Lee tried to scare her by growling like a bear again.

"Will you be *quiet*?" Frankie said. She felt frightened already, and her brother was just making it worse. She thought back to what Damien and her dad had said about bears, and that made her feel calmer.

Adam opened a sandwich and **recoiled**, pretending to be horrified. "What's that green stuff?" he asked.

"Sprouts," Lee said glumly. "They taste like grass, or maybe hay."

"Your dad thinks we're horses," Adam said, neighing and pawing at the ground like a horse. The other boys howled with laughter.

"That's not funny," Frankie muttered. "Hanging out with Lee has really **skewed** your sense of humor, Adam."

STOP AND CHECK

Why was Frankie anxious about the hike?

Chapter 3 The Accident

They started hiking again right after lunch. Frankie got behind, but Dad made sure that she was near the group at all times. When they came to a big rock, they stopped to rest. Frankie's boots felt hot and uncomfortable, and she had a blister on her heel.

Frankie stuck a bandage on her blister. She watched Adam climbing the rock, followed by Lee and Damien. Dad carefully pulled himself up after the boys. But when Dad reached the top, part of the rock crumbled, and he lost his balance and fell. He landed awkwardly and very hard.

Frankie shouted for Lee, and he quickly but carefully climbed back to the ground.

Dad had his right arm crossed over his chest, holding on to his left shoulder. His face was such a mask of pain that Frankie had trouble looking at him.

"Dad?" she said. "Dad, are you all right?"

"I'm okay," he **murmured**. He spoke so softly that Frankie could hardly hear him.

Lee wanted to help Dad up, but Frankie stopped him. "We don't know what's wrong yet," she said. "It looks like his shoulder, but it could also be his neck or his back."

"It's my shoulder," Dad said **feebly**. "My head hurts, too, but it's not as bad."

Frankie knew she needed to take charge, and almost immediately, she felt a new calmness and strength.

"We need the survival blanket," Frankie told the boys firmly. "It's that silver blanket in Dad's backpack. People in shock get cold, and the blanket keeps them warm."

"How do you know that?" Lee asked.

STOP AND CHECK

How does Frankie respond to the accident?

"I read about hiking safety yesterday," Frankie said. "It's important to keep Dad warm, still, and comfortable."

"I'll go get help," Adam said. "We passed a ranger station on the way to the trail."

Dad **roused** himself and sat up to speak, but the effort was too much for him. He had to lie back down quickly. Frankie realized that he probably needed water and painkillers.

Adam started **rummaging** through the supplies in Dad's backpack. "I found the map," he said, unfolding it. "Look, here's a shortcut. It's not a marked trail, but I can follow one of these streams if I get lost. There are lots of them."

Frankie didn't think Adam's plan was a good one. She didn't remember seeing lots of streams on their hike, only two. She **peered** at the map, looking closely over Adam's shoulder.

"Those lines aren't streams; they're contour lines that show the shape of the land," she told him.

"Contour lines show how high you are above sea level," she continued. "Dad showed me when we looked at the map back in the parking lot."

"It still looks like a quicker route to me," Adam said.

Frankie knew she had to **summon** the courage to stop Adam. Otherwise, he might turn their **dilemma** into a disaster. "If you get hurt or lost, Dad won't be rescued," she said.

No one spoke for a long time.

Finally, Damien broke the silence. "Frankie's right," he said. "It's safer to go back the way we came."

Dad groaned, and Frankie felt fear run through her like a jolt of electricity. Someone needed to leave to get help now, and she needed to take care of her father. But there was no way she was staying there alone. She hadn't forgotten about the bears.

"One of you has to stay with me," she said calmly. "We should split into two groups of two for safety."

"Let me guess—you read that, too?" Adam said, but Damien quickly said that Frankie's idea made sense.

They decided that Lee and Adam would go get help and Damien and Frankie would stay behind. Frankie made sure that Lee and Adam had food, water, and the map with them.

There wasn't much to do after Lee and Adam left. Frankie adjusted the blanket around her dad and gave him water regularly, while Damien watched for Lee and Adam's return.

Before long, Lee and Adam returned with a park ranger. The ranger checked on Dad and said that he'd be fine.

"It's lucky that I was on the trail today," the ranger said. "I used my radio to call for a helicopter, and it will be here soon."

Then the ranger turned to Frankie and said, "Your father is lucky that you were here today. Your brother told me you took charge and stayed calm." Lee smiled at her.

Frankie smiled shyly and said, "I'm not very good with bears, but I found out that I can use what I've learned to make the right decisions."

STOP AND CHECK

How does Frankie use what she knows about maps to help them out of the situation?

Summarize

Summarize how a challenge changed Frankie. Use important details from *Bear Country*. Your graphic organizer may help you.

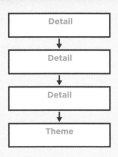

Text Evidence

1. Reread page 5. How does Frankie deal with her worry about the hike? THEME

2. Find the word *contour* on page 12. What clues help you figure out the word's meaning? VOCABULARY

3. Write about what Frankie does in Chapter 3. How do her actions show what the author's main message is? WRITE ABOUT READING

Compare Texts

Read about a girl who met a challenge.

I knew I shouldn't do it, but I was with friends—or people I wanted as friends. They made bad ideas seem like good ideas.

Laura, Rachel, Emily, and I were about to play a game called "Who Can Stay on the Phone the Longest." It sounded easy, but there was a rule that made it hard. The person I called had to be a complete stranger. Laura held the record for the longest call at five minutes, forty seconds.

It was my turn, and I was terrified. I'd never made a prank call before, and I didn't want to start now.

Rachel gave me a sympathetic look and asked, "Do you want a glass of milk?"

I shook my head because the thought of eating or drinking anything made me feel sick.

Laura held out the phone and raised her eyebrows. She was the leader of the group and she was used to telling everyone what to do. Last semester, I hadn't cared what Laura thought of me because I had my best friend, Nina. Now Nina went to a different school, and I felt alone.

I wiped my hands on my jeans and reached for the phone. I had made my decision. The phone rang, and a familiar voice answered right away.

"Hey, Nina," I said, "it's me..."

I finished my conversation with Nina ten minutes later. "You broke the rules," Laura said. "We all called strangers."

"I couldn't do it," I said. "I think it's a bad idea."

"Actually," Rachel said, "I haven't done it either, and Emily hung up after two seconds."

"I didn't want to upset a stranger," Emily said. "I agree that it's a stupid game."

Laura didn't say anything, but she seemed uncertain. Then she surprised me by nodding and changing the subject. "What's Nina's new school like?" she asked.

"Okay," I said, "but she doesn't know anyone yet."

"You must really miss each other," Laura said.

"Well, you have us now," Rachel said.

"Totally true," Emily added.

And maybe I did.

Make Connections

How did the narrator's decision change her challenging situation? ESSENTIAL QUESTION

Compare how Frankie in *Bear Country* and the girl in *The Call* speak up for what they know is right. TEXT TO TEXT

Focus on Literary Elements

Simile A simile is a way of describing one thing by comparing it with something else. Authors use similes to make vivid descriptions. When you're reading, a simile can help you better understand what is being described.

Read and Find Similes often have the words *like* or *as*. Here are some examples: *He turned red as a beet. She swam like a dolphin. Joey was as quiet as a mouse.*

On page 5 of *Bear Country*, the author writes that the trail "disappeared into the forest like a path in a fairy tale."

Your Turn

Have a simile challenge with a partner or in a group. Set a time limit, such as five minutes. Look for other similes in the story.

When the time is up, read the similes you have found to each other. Check that they have the words *like* or *as*.